I am a
Camel

Karen Durrie

www.av2books.com

Go to **www.av2books.com**, and enter this book's unique code.

BOOK CODE

U385634

AV² by Weigl brings you media enhanced books that support active learning.

AV² provides enriched content that supplements and complements this book. Weigl's AV² books strive to create inspired learning and engage young minds in a total learning experience.

Your AV² Media Enhanced books come alive with...

Audio
Listen to sections of the book read aloud.

Key Words
Study vocabulary, and complete a matching word activity.

Video
Watch informative video clips.

Quizzes
Test your knowledge.

Embedded Weblinks
Gain additional information for research.

Slide Show
View images and captions, and prepare a presentation.

Try This!
Complete activities and hands-on experiments.

... and much, much more!

Published by AV² by Weigl
350 5th Avenue, 59th Floor New York, NY 10118
Website: www.av2books.com www.weigl.com

Library of Congress Cataloging-in-Publication Data

Durrie, Karen.
 I am a camel / Karen Durrie. -- 1st ed.
    p. cm. -- (I am)
 Includes bibliographical references and index.
 ISBN 978-1-61913-231-3 (hardcover : alk. paper) -- ISBN 978-1-61913-232-0 (softcover : alk. paper)
 1. Camels--Juvenile literature. I. Title.
 QL737.U54D87 2013
 599.63'62--dc23
                              2011042510

Printed in the United States of America in North Mankato, Minnesota
1 2 3 4 5 6 7 8 9 0 16 15 14 13 12

012012
WEP060112

Project Coordinator: Karen Durrie Art Director: Terry Paulhus

Weigl acknowledges Getty Images as the primary image supplier for this title.

I am a Camel

In this book, I will teach you about

- myself
- my food
- my home
- my family

and much more!

I am a camel.

5

I have a hump on my back.
It is made of fat.

I can drink 227 bottles of water in 10 minutes.

9

I do not have a hump when I am born.

11

I have two rows
of eye lashes
and three eyelids.

13

I have hair that can be made into wool.

15

I yell, kick, and spit when I am upset.

I can carry 220 pounds on my back.

I live in herds kept by people.

I am a camel.

21

CAMEL FACTS

These pages provide detailed information that expands on the interesting facts found in the book. They are intended to be used by adults as a learning support to help young readers round out their knowledge of each amazing animal featured in the I Am series.

Pages 4–5

I am a camel. Camels have long legs and necks, and small heads. Their feet have two toes, which spread out to keep the camels from sinking in sand. Camels live in the hot desert climates of northern Africa and southwestern Asia. They were introduced to Australia in the 1800s when explorers brought them to use as helping animals.

Pages 6–7

Camels have humps on their backs made of fat. There are two types of camels. The Bactrian has two humps, and the Arabian, or dromedary, has one hump. A camel's hump can store up to 80 pounds (36 kilograms) of fat, which can be broken down into water and energy if there is no food around.

Pages 8–9

Camels can drink 227 bottles of water in 10 minutes. Camels can drink up to 30 gallons (113.5 liters) of water in 10 minutes. That is as much water as a person drinks in about 55 days. Camels normally need about 5 to 10 gallons (19 to 38 L) of water a day, but they can go long periods without drinking any water.

Pages 10–11

Camels do not have humps when they are born. Once camel calves begin to eat solid food, they grow a hump. Baby camels drink their mother's milk, and then they begin to eat grass when they are two or three months old.

Pages 12–13

Camels have two rows of eyelashes and three eyelids.
Camels have many ways of protecting their bodies from the blowing sand in the desert. Two rows of eyelashes and a thin third eyelid keep sand and dust out of the camel's eyes. Camels can also close their nostrils to keep sand out of their nose.

Pages 14–15

Camels have hair that can be made into wool.
Camels have lighter coats when it is warm. They grow thicker, woollier coats when the weather is cool. Camels shed their coats in big clumps. Their hair can be spun into soft wool that is used to make clothing and rugs.

Pages 16–17

Camels yell, kick, and spit when they are upset.
Camels are usually calm animals, but if they are annoyed or feel threatened, they may bite or kick. They are well known for spitting when angry or excited. They bring up contents of their stomach to spit at whatever is bothering them.

Pages 18–19

Camels can carry 220 pounds on their back.
Camels are used to carry loads long distances. They can also be ridden. Dromedary camels can carry up to 220 pounds (100 kg) on their backs for about 37 miles (60 kilometers), while Bactrian camels are able to carry 440 pounds (200 kg) for 31 miles (50 km).

Pages 20–21

Camels live in herds kept by people.
Camels are very social animals and like to be with other camels. Camels are mostly kept as helping animals. There are almost no wild camels left in the world. Wild Arabian camels are extinct, and wild Bactrians are endangered, with only about 950 left in the Gobi Desert in Asia.

WORD LIST

Research has shown that as much as 65 percent of all written material published in English is made up of 300 words. These 300 words cannot be taught using pictures or learned by sounding them out. They must be recognized by sight. This book contains 29 common sight words to help young readers improve their reading fluency and comprehension. This book also teaches young readers several important content words, such as proper nouns. These words are paired with pictures to aid in learning and improve understanding.

Page	Sight Words First Appearance	Page	Content Words First Appearance
4	a, am, I	4	camel
6	back, have, is, it, made, my, of, on	6	fat, hump
8	can, in, water	8	bottles, minutes
10	do, not, when	12	eyelids, lashes, rows
12	and, eye, three, two	14	hair, wool
14	be, into, that	16	upset
18	carry	18	pounds
20	by, live, people	20	herds

24